# Inspirational Quotes from remarkable Women and Girls

*Provide motivation and inspiration for your daily challenges*

JAMEKA WATKINS

ISBN: 9781660041138

# DEDICATION

Life is too short for us to grasp all the values in life, so the question of how we should live to achieve ourselves to the fullest has become a dilemma. Hope that this book with some great quotes will bring you useful things to lay the foundation of your lifestyle, as well as sowing you seeds of spiritual life in order to nurture better living habits every day.

# CONTENTS



"With the new day comes new strength and new thoughts".-Eleanor Roosevelt



"Every great dream begins with a dreamer."- Harriet Tubman



"Just don't give up trying to do what you really want to do. Where there is love and inspiration, I don't think you can go wrong."- Ella Fitzgerald



"The most important thing is to enjoy your life- to be happy- it's all that matters."- Audrey Hepburn



"I really think a champion is defined not by their wins but by how they can recover when they fall."- Serena Williams



"It's one of the greatest gifts you can give yourself, to forgive. Forgive everybody."-Maya Angelou.



"Success is only meaningful and enjoyable if it feels like your own."- Michelle Obama



"Learn to value yourself, which means: fight for your happiness."- Ayn Rand

# MINDSET SEEDS
## Everyday Inspiration


This book will show how philosophy can help to improve your thinking about everyday life. And by improving the quality of your thinking, you can improve the quality of your life. It will make you more aware of what you think and why—and how you can change what you think

Looking for just the right words to inspire yourself or your daughter, sister, mother, female teammate or girlfriend? The Beautiful Quotes Making Up Mindset is a perfect gift for personal inspiration gallery filled with several beautiful quotes...and, the stories behind the wise words. Within many themed chapters are women and girls who believe, build, discover, explore, heal, invent, laugh and lead. It's a collection that's designed to be shared. So passions get sparked and role models emerge.

You'll love discovering quotes by unforgettable women from bygone eras including Eleanor Roosevelt, Ella Fitzgerald, Harriet Tubman and Audrey Hepburn as well as contemporary heroines like Serena Williams, Amy Poehler and Malala Yousafzai. They are great stars among the noteworthy up-and-comers...

Make up your mindset from the formers' seeds.

"If you can't become the princess of someone,
let yourself be the queen of your life"

# 1.  SEED 1ST

## KEEP EVERYTHING SIMPLE

**"With the new day comes new strength and new thoughts."- Eleanor Roosevelt**

What's My Life's Purpose?
Countless people ponder this question... I certainly did. It took quite a bit of self-exploration, many months of research, and a lot of trial and error to help me arrive at a clear conclusion. But, it did happen; and when it finally clicked together, it was as though I found the secret to happiness.

My life became far more meaningful and fulfilling, and I enjoyed more free time as well as better overall health. And, you can experience this, too.
It's so simple that we are completing our misson the God gives each of us. Become a good cell for whole life as well a colorful piece of a giant life's picture. Take, Eleanor's diary, as a typical example

"Needless to say, the big thing in the past twenty-four hours has been the Supreme Court decision. I thought it was going to be the budget, but that has been completely overshadowed. It seemed to me that after a long afternoon of reading and rereading and trying to thoroughly digest legal opinions, we would have a rather quiet and subdued swim at six o'clock. One of our sons who was still home, a young friend of his, and one of the men who has been working with my husband, all appeared with me at the pool.

My husband was already in the water and before I reached the door, I dropped my wrapper, plunged into the water, and swimming about very quietly, I inquired hesitatingly how they were all feeling. To my complete surprise instead of either discouragement or even annoyance, I was told that everyone was feeling fine, and on that note we finished our swim, went up to dress for dinner and the family met again at the dinner table, no guests were present.

I was prepared for some candid opinions on current events. Instead I found that we were discussing history. My memory for dates is extremely bad, but between us we settled the dates of the dark ages, the middle ages, the Renaissance and how long the Holy Roman Empire remained a reality and when it continued in name but was really only a figment of the imagination. Then we took up what happened in the different countries during the Renaissance, and reluctantly we got up from the table at a quarter past nine, still violently discussing the history of the past when I imagine most supper or dinner tables which gave any thought at all to questions of government discussed those of the present day.

My husband plunged into work on a speech and I went off to work on an article. Midnight came and bed for all, and all that was said was "good night, sleep well, pleasant dreams, with the new day comes new strength and new thoughts."

Your own life's purpose is by taking the complicated and breaking it down into a simple process.

This is a place in your mind where you can find answers to all the questions in your life - answers that will actually help you overcome any limitations that are keeping you from your goals.
Break the secret to living happily. I get it. 'What's my life's purpose?' is a pretty hefty question. But, the answer is actually a lot simpler than most people can imagine.

The secret to living a fulfilling and happy life is all about how you view your life's limitations -- and having the right tools to overcome them.

Keeping everything simple will give you the power to turn any limitation you may be facing into an opportunity that is achievable. With this framework I was able to change my life so that I'm living it on my terms, and my goal is to teach you how to develop a simple framework that will help you overcome just about any limitation that stands in your way.

This morning I woke up to my new (rainy) day. My initial thought when I looked out the window was yuck, rain! I could have allowed this thought to occupy my mindset all day long, but instead, I decided to reframe that old way of thinking into a new thought: Yes! It's not snowing! Shortly after arriving to the gym, I realized I was missing a $20 bill I had brought with me, which must've been lost amidst the chaos of trying to avoid the rain. My first thought was disappointment.

However, that thought also quickly changed to hope and faith: I'll find it, I thought. I retraced my steps and scoured the gym floors… to no avail. On the way out, I asked the front desk if they had seen any misplaced cash… I think you can guess what their answer was–YES! If I had let that initial thought of disappointment dictate my actions when I first realized I had lost my $20 who knows if I would have even bothered to search for it. If I had let the initial disappointment in the weather take hold of my energy, who knows if I would have even made it to the gym this morning. Thought management happens all day as a daily basic.

What do you need to do more of or less of to believe in yourself and to believe in others? Just be yourself to choose what you need, don't care more thoughts of others because you have the only life to live.

So many big arguments begin with small comments. How many times have you started a conversation on friendly terms, then wound up in some kind of dispute that you didn't anticipate?

In my work as a family, divorce, and small-claims mediator, I've seen countless offhand remarks start a fight or add fuel to an existing fire. And I have found myself in plenty of situations where I've wanted to give someone (my husband, a colleague) what I thought was helpful advice only to inadvertently offend him or her.

The holidays, with all their extended-family gatherings, can be a verbal minefield. You're either dodging nosy questions from some tactless relative over dinner ("Still dieting then?") or taking out the stress of all that extra cooking and shopping on those dearest to you ("Do I have to do everything around here?").

Each stage of life is the most beautiful stage if we know how to live life to the fullest and appreciate every moment of life. Time does not wait for anyone. Therefore, do not keep in mind that: "I will do it tomorrow".

Life is full of uncertainties, no one can predict what will happen tomorrow. Cherish every moment of living and doing your best you will not have to shed tears of regret. Living your best is also a way to pay for what you deserve.

*How beautiful life would be when we keep everything simple*

# 2. SEED 2<sup>ND</sup>

## KEEP YOUR DREAM

**"Every great dream begins with a dreamer."- Harriet Tubman**


Known as the "Moses of her people," Harriet Tubman was enslaved, escaped, and helped others gain their freedom as a "conductor" of the Underground Railroad. Tubman also served as a scout, spy, guerrilla soldier, and nurse for the Union Army during the Civil War. She is considered the first African American woman to serve in the military.

"Every great dream begins with a dreamer. Always remember, you have within you the strength, the patience, and the passion to reach for the stars to change the world."

Dreaming is something like....wake up each morning with hope and wishes....you want to further for....its boosting for today...for better tomorrow experiencing yesterday woes..... Every human being has the capability to dream - as long as we can imagine our next step, the stars are within reach.

One person can change the world. No matter what you are suffering, it's possible to emerge with passion, strength and patience. Your dream has the power to change the world. Right now, think about the people who will be impacted because of your decision to pursue what matters most to you. Literally see them in your mind's eye and see how their life will be different because you went for something so much bigger than you ever imagined.

The thing is, that dream is not your dream. It is Spirit's request to you to discover the strength, the passion and the patience that is designed into your very being. But, it is only when you reach for what seems like the impossible that you discover just how magnificent you truly are. And as you discover that, you unlock a power that truly changes the world.

According my neighborhood, seventeen years ago, on May 12th, 1999, my then-boyfriend followed her on a family trip to Ireland and proposed at Ross Castle in Killarney. Her cheeks were sore from smiling and She couldn't wait to begin the next chapter of her life. It was like a dream come true.

Since then She had learned that the marriage is so much more important than the wedding day, that you fall in and out of like and love on a daily basis, and that having kids challenges you to the breaking point and rewards you with epic joy.

Becoming a mother made her more aware of how my attitude and choices might steer those whose ears were listening and eyes were watching.

One day her 10-year-old son said to her, "In my opinion, you are a dreamer and dad is a realist. But you need both, you know?" "Why is that," She asked? "Well because without the dreamer, the realist would never get off the ground. And without the realist, the dreamer might go too far."

She thinks he's right. But many of us have too much realism and not enough dream. Dreaming is the first thing to go when life gets tough. When the focus needs to be on the bills and the meals and the list of things that must get done.

However, dreaming is also what helps raise us up to a better place. Where we can follow our heart and make a difference.

As Harriet Tubman said, "Every great dream begins with a dreamer. Always remember, you have within you the strength, the patience, and the passion to reach for the stars to change the world."

And Langston Hughes said, "Hold fast to dreams, for if dreams die, life is a broken-winged bird that cannot fly."

The journey She began seventeen years ago has been filled with many different dreams. Dreams of being a mother, a writer, and an agent of change. Dreams of becoming more of myself. Every day She try to take one more step in that direction.

*Dreams never die.*
*Keep your dream and it will become true someday.*

# 3. SEED 3<sup>RD</sup>

## BE CONFIDDENT

**"Just don't give up trying to do what you really want to do. Where there is love and inspiration, I don't think you can go wrong."- Ella Fitzgerald**

Known as "the First Lady of Song," Ella Fitzgerald was a famous jazz singer and the first African-American woman to win a Grammy Award.

After a troubled childhood anchored in many financial problems, Ella entered her name for a dance contest. That's right! Her first dream was to become a dancer. But at the time, the odds were not in Ella's favor.
When she noticed another group of performers, she knew she couldn't really compete with them, so she decided to sing instead. And it was a life-changing decision. The crowd was amazed; she won the first prize and soon became a singer in Chick Webb's band. From that moment on, Ella Fitzgerald was a constant success. Her beautiful voice won her no less than 13 Grammys and sold her more than 40 million albums.

A strong-willed woman who came from nothing, Ella Fitzgerald was and remains a jazz legend. Here are 12 beautiful Ella Fitzgerald quotes on love and all the things that really count in life.

Her quote is a tribute to her own hard work. If you really want something, you should just keep working at it. If you're following your heart and doing what inspires you, you're sure to succeed eventually. Ella Fitzgerald knew this was easier said than done, but that didn't mean she would ever give up. Will you?

If someone is thinking of calling it quits, you might want to think about breaking out this perfect little inspirational gem. Never surrender! Follow your dreams! And all that jazz! If you were to drop this quote at a dinner party, would you get an in-unison "awww" or would everyone roll their eyes and never invite you back? Here it is, on a scale of 1-10.


Sure, people may roll their eyes a little because you're a starry-eyed dreamer, but don't listen to them. You dream your dreams…and you make sure to "accidentally" lose their contact info when you make it to the big time.

Someday, someone asked me that

"Do you think it is wrong to hold an opinion?" .

To say that it is wrong or right would merely be another opinion, wouldn't it? But if one begins to observe and understand how opinions are formed, then perhaps one may be able to perceive the actual significance of opinion, judgment, agreement. Thought is the result of influence, isn't it? Your thinking and your opinions are dictated by the way you have been brought up. You say, 'This is right, that is wrong,' according to the moral pattern of your particular conditioning. We are not for the moment concerned with what is true beyond all influence, or whether there is such truth. We are trying to see the significance of opinions, beliefs, assertions, whether they be collective or personal. Opinion, belief, agreement or disagreement, are responses according to one's background narrow or wide. Isn't that so?

"Yes, but is that wrong?"

Again, if you say it is right or wrong, you are still in the field of opinions. Truth is not a matter of opinion; a fact does not depend on agreement or belief. You and I may agree to call this object a watch, but by any other name it would still be what it is. Your belief or opinion is something that has been given to you by the society in which you live. In revolting against it, as a reaction, you may form a different opinion, another belief; but you are still on the same level, aren't you?

You have certain ideas and opinions about love, haven't you?

"Yes."

How did you get them?

'I have read what the saints and the great religious teachers have said about love, and having thought it over I have formed my own conclusions.'
Which are shaped by your likes and dislikes, are they not? You like or you don't like what others have said about love, and you decide which statement is right and which is wrong according to your own predilection.

"I choose that which I consider to be true."

On what is your choice based?

"On my own knowledge and discernment."

What do you mean by knowledge? I am not trying to trip or corner you but together we are trying to understand why we have opinions, ideas and conclusions about love. If once we understand this, we can go very much more deeply into the matter. So, what do you mean by knowledge?

"People are their most beautiful when they are laughing, crying, dancing, playing, telling the truth, and being chased in a fun way."- Amy Poehler

**Just be yourself, gain confidence with what you chose because it's personal choice and there is no right or wrong here. Just be worth or not.**

If you *Believe* in yourself
*Anything* is possible

# 4. SEED 4<sup>TH</sup>

# ENJOY YOUR LIFE

**"The most important thing is to enjoy your life- to be happy- it's all that matters."- Audrey Hepburn**

Yes, the most important thing in life is to be happy. By this way you all those things which you do will be great. If we always are happy in life then we find out that life is wonderful and full of joy.

In this world, those people achieve the most who always be happy. It the rules of life because once you live happy life things are going to change. In today world it is also important to be happy because without it you cannot do the thing you want with your full potential.

It varies from person to person to do what makes them happy. Some become happy by helping others while for some it is all about traveling.

In today's world, we see many people are unhappy because they are not doing what they love. We live our life on the expectation of others. Sometimes we make other people happy by sacrificing our own happiness. But in the end the things that matter is to make yourself happy first.

We live in the era of social media where we see others happiness any try to chase they're a way of happiness. In this, we are fall in more problem than before. Because each and every person has a different way to be happy. By happiness, we find our life more joyful and miserable.

Some of the people expect more than they do from life and it the major problem to get unhappy. When you listen to some successful people out there that all say do what you love. To make life more meaning full we must do the thing which makes ourselves happy.

Do those things that are important to you. So, if we want to be happy in life. We must do what makes us happy as well as meaning full to ourselves.

Let yourself try what you have never tried before such as yoga. This kind of sports is a combination between breaths and body movements. Try once to listen to your soul, flow your mind with waves on some beaches.  There are no strangers here; only friends you haven't yet met. Every day you are surrounded by kind and generous acts; freely given without expectations. The property grounds are a source of so much beauty and serenity. Especially for those who are able to free their minds and spirits from agitation, to leave superficiality and things which are not authentic aside, to fully embrace the peace found in gazing at the ocean and allowing the crooning of its waves to lull you. Worries and fears are lost; love takes over behavior patterns. Without being aware of it, a smile settles on your face.

If you crave spiritual joy, and the opportunity to leave a place feeling that something has changed inside you, making you aware of how much we have to be grateful for, please consider try something new.

We are all here to live, but our individual missions aren't always the same. Some are explorers, searching for adventure in all that they do. Others choose to build a life of service through innovation and creativity. There is truly no shortage of destinies, roles or dreams to fill; we're a planet of healers, givers, teachers... Thinking of better goals starts building your philosophy- your own meaning of life.

Life is too short to brood over the things of the past. If we want to live happily and peacefully we must practice the art of living. Art of living teaches us to enjoy every moment and be happy. After all that is all what matters!

Personally, one of the biggest reasons why I love life is because of echo in our hearts. So whether it's for self-motivation, your next t-shirt design or simply for your Instagram bio, this collection of short quotes is full of powerful ideas packed into tiny little packages of words. They have made a profound positive impact in my life and I'm sure they will make one in yours as well.

The bamboo tower buckled under the wind but then burst up proudly as if nothing had happened. Each of us carries in us the character of the bamboo. That's for sure.

Stumbling is not the way for you to give up your dreams and hopes. This is an "opportunity" for you to look at yourself and learn from experience for next time. Change your attitude after each failure. Time doesn't wait for anyone but it's never too late. The beginning or the end is your own

Life is too short to worry about unworth things, enjoy any second in our life as if it's the last day. Because it is the greatest present the God gave us.

LIFE IS
BETTER
WHEN
YOU'RE
LAUGHING

# 5. SEED 5<sup>TH</sup>

## KEEP LEARNING

**"I really think a champion is defined not by their wins but by how they can recover when they fall."- Serena Williams**

As well known as a great tenis player with timeless quotes, Serena gave us some remarkable lessons in which never give up and keep yourself learning is one of the most meaningful pages. With a defeat, when you lose, you get up, you make it better, you try again. That's what we do in life, when we get down, when we get sick, we don't want to just stop. We keep going and try to do more. Everyone always says never give up but you really have to take that to heart and really do never definitely give up."

Probably curiosity with some is a beautiful aspect. No matter which names we give them—God, Universe, fate. It changes nothing. Believers who claim someone has a better plan for us still look for the consolation. They keep searching for the reasons for the mess in their lives, and they find it in something incomprehensible—mysterious and powerful creatures that manage their lives. The work is done. Now they can keep wallowing in self-pity and waiting for a windfall to come.

Stop deluding yourself. There is no purpose of our existence at the scale of the universe. We are the fruits of our parent's love.

Do not exaggerate your mission; accept the life you got and learn to appreciate it.
Learn from the world around us, from family, relatives, friends and even failure. Sometimes, what happens in our life is not as good as we expect but everything also has their own reasons. And we just wait the time in place. Family gives us moral lessons since we were children. School makes us broaden our horizon with complicated curriculum, Maths, Science, Physic, etc. Even our ex, they also send an expensive lesson, which sometimes we have to pay by our youth to relieve all things. Our teachers, maybe we owe them the "thank you" for teach me how to mature in love, to become a real adult who know respect what we have.

Knowledge is infinite. We spend most of our time learning and it's also probable our mission. We learn on purpose or sometimes, we learn unconsciously. Friends can come and go, but what each of them gave in our life means a page of experiences. Respect what they have taught us because thanks to them, we mature gradually.

Learn to be better, because success comes when we become our better version than yesterday.

The best thing is that Learning from Failure:
"I don't like to lose-at anything… Yet I've grown most not from victories, but setbacks. If winning is God's reward, then losing is how he teaches us."
– Serena Williams

According to some people lessons that we learn from our life through various experiences are enough to ensure our success. I do agree with this view to a certain extent. Some of the most successful people in the world received no formal schooling and yet they made a name for themselves by learning from their mistakes and constantly improving their strategies. However, there are only a handful of such people and the vast majority of successful people that we see today are highly educated. In my opinion, formal schooling is as important as life lessons for ensuring the success of a person.

There are certainly a lot of things that we can learn from our life. Life experiences teach us to constantly improve our game by learning from our mistakes. For example, some of the most successful businessmen, politicians and sportspersons of this and the previous century received hardly any formal education. However, they did not waste even a single opportunity to learn from their mistakes and constantly upped their game. Obviously, life lessons can help us succeed.

On the other hand, very few people manage to succeed on the merit of the lessons they learned from life. The vast majority of successful people that we know today have fancy degrees from reputed international institutions. In this age of information explosion, academic learning is all the more important. Companies no longer recruit people who lack a degree. Hence, it is foolish to believe that life lessons alone will ensure our success in life and career.

In conclusion, lessons that we learn from our experiences are certainly important and play a crucial role in making us successful. However, today we need formal education as well because most of the opportunities are in the skilled sector and someone who lacks a university degree cannot seize them. Learn to love. Love unconditionally. Have you ever done that? Or always just want others to love you, want to "receive" everything but not "let" go at all? It is said that giving is far better than taking and it is truth.
Life is wonderful, no one has everything but no one loses everything. The pain will be greatly eased if healed by love. Love is spreading your arms to the wonderful emotions brought about by life.

The most important thing is not to read these things, but our attitudes and opinions to the things that life brings. Let those "priceless gifts" of life cool your soul, let you live better and enjoy miraculous happiness!
Each day passed is each new thing we learn. Learn to be stronger. Learn to gain confident and explore our limit- it is endless.

# 6. SEED 6TH

## FORGIVE AND FORGET

**"It's one of the greatest gifts you can give yourself, to forgive. Forgive everybody."-Maya Angelou.**

Is the bravest
The first to forgive
Is the strongest
First to forget
Is the happiest
This is the hardest thing to do but so true

When you forgive others you set yourself free.

It is a spiritual law that we experience what we intend for others. When we want to experience forgiveness then it really helps to offer forgiveness. The practise of forgiving other people for the hurts which they hurt us; is one of the most effective ways to experience being forgiven for the ways in which we have hurt others - and to makes it less likely that we will make the same mistakes again.

You benefit immensely when you choose to forgive and so does everyone around you. Whether you need to forgive others, or need to forgive yourself, doing so sets you free from the past and enables you to fulfil your true potential. Forgiveness allows you to break free from limiting beliefs and attitudes. It frees up your mental and emotional energies so that you can apply them to creating a better life.

Forgiveness helps you achieve even your most practical and immediate goals. Perhaps you want a better job, to earn more money, have better relationships, or live in a nicer place. Forgiveness helps you achieve all of these. If you have not forgiven then a part of your inner life energy is trapped in resentment, anger, pain, or suffering of some kind. This trapped life energy will limit you. It it like trying to ride a bicycle with the brakes partly on all the time. It slows you down, frustrates you and makes it difficult to move forward.

The choices you make and the things that you believe are possible will all be influenced by the ways you have not forgiven. As you learn to forgive the energy which was going into unhappy thoughts and feelings gets liberated and can flow into creating the life you want rather than limiting you, or creating more suffering.

If you do not want to learn to forgive to benefit yourself; then learn to forgive so you can benefit others. As you learn to forgive you benefit everyone you are in contact with. Your thinking will be clearer and more positive than before. You will have a lot more to give and you will more readily enjoy sharing what you have. You will naturally and easily become kinder, more generous and more caring of others - without having to struggle to achieve this. You will have a happier and more positive attitude to the people in your life and they will respond more positively to you in return.

Is a forgiving person easier to be around than an unforgiving one? Yes, of course they are. A forgiving person is always much easier to be around than an unforgiving one. The quality of your life depends on the quality of your relationships. Every aspect of your life will change for the better as you learn to forgive; whether in your family, your work life or your social life. Learning to forgive will improve all your relationships, because your attitude will improve. As your relationships improve, then all aspects of your life will also improve.

If you want to move up to the next level of financial abundance and success, Forgiveness will help you achieve it. For example, if you want more money in your life you need to make sure that you do not resent people who have more money than you. People with more money than you are the ones best placed to help you have more money too. If, as some people do, you resent "people with money" then they will not be able to help you, because you are not open to them while you are busy resenting them. Likewise, if you have a positive attitude to people who are more successful than you (you smile at them rather than glower at them) they will see you as approachable and will more likely want to work with you, or socialise with you.

If you want a better job, and to earn more money, then having a positive attitude towards the place you work, towards your boss, towards colleagues and towards clients or customers, helps immensely. People who have a positive, helpful attitude stand out in any situation. You can never succeed in an organisation which you do not want to succeed, because you will not give of your best. If you do not give of your best, by doing the best job you can, then you will not receive the best that can come to you. Forgiveness will help you have the kind of attitude which will make you very successful at your job.

Learning to forgive yourself is vitally important too. Hurting yourself, by refusing to forgive yourself, hurts others also. If you do not forgive yourself then you will punish yourself by denying yourself the good things in life. The more you deny yourself the less you have to give. The less you have to give the less you can benefit those around you. When you stop limiting what you receive then you stop limiting what you can give. Everyone benefits when you forgive yourself as you then allow better into your life, and have a lot more to share.

When you forgive; you become a better husband or wife, you become a better student or teacher, you become a better employer or employee and you become a better parent or child. When you forgive you are more open to success in whatever ways are meaningful to you. As you learn to forgive, what seemed impossible not only becomes possible, but can even become easily achievable.

If you are a religious, or spiritually minded, person then learning practical ways to forgive will enhance and deepen your experience of your religion or spiritual practice. It will help free you from guilt about not being as "good" as you feel you should be, because it will help you become the type of person you would like to be. Practising forgiveness strengthens the goodness within you so that it becomes more active in your life. You will naturally feel less inclined to do the things you know you should not do, but have not been able to stop yourself doing. You will start to do more of the things you know you ought to do, but have not been able to get yourself to do.

Learning to forgive can only help you; it cannot hurt you.

Forgiveness is immensely practical and helpful. There is nothing vague, or impractical about it. Forgiveness sets you free. As you learn to forgive many problems (possibly even health problems) will gradually disappear. It will be as if you can view your life from above and can see the easiest way get to where you want to be. Life will open up in front of you. New opportunities will emerge as if from nowhere. Happy coincides will occur where you meet just the right person at just the right time. Ideas or answers will come to you just as you need them. A friend may make a comment, or you flip open a book or a magazine, or you may overhear a conversation which gives you just what you were looking for. Why is this so? It is because by practising forgiveness you become more open to the goodness of life, so that goodness is more able to find its way to you.

As you learn to forgive, abilities which have been dormant within you will emerge, and you will discover yourself to be a much stronger and more capable person than you previously imagined. Parts of yourself which could not thrive in the frigid soil of unforgiveness will start to grow. You will begin to let go of struggling and striving. You will find more of an easy flow and life will be a lot more pleasant and a lot more enjoyable. If this all sounds like exaggeration, then let that be for now. Simply practice the Four Steps to Forgiveness that you will find within these pages and you will be very glad that you did.
Forgiving is easier said than done.

Most people believe that forgiveness means condoning an event. But it's not. Blame ties us to the past and makes our heart and mind smaller—both literally and metaphorically. Forgiving, on the other hand, means realizing that resentment and hatred add more pain.

Science shows that forgiving is good for your health.

You can't change the past. There's nothing you can do to remove the harm others might have caused you. However, not forgiving damages our mood—we see our lives through a lens of vengeance, hostility, resentment, anger, and sadness.

Forgiveness was traditionally seen as a religious ideal; science has turned it into a skill that everyone can (and should) develop. From 1998 to 2005, the number of empirical studies on the topic has increased from 58 to 950. There's been a lot of progress understanding the science behind forgiveness.

Holding a severe grudge raises our blood pressure and increases our chances of a heart attack. Unforgiveness intensifies mental problems, such as depression, anxiety, and post-traumatic stress disorders.

An fMRI study by Italian researcher, Dr. Pietro Pietrini, showed that anger and vengeance inhibited rational thinking. Conversely, the tasks involved in the process of forgiveness activate the areas of our brain linked to problem-solving, morality, empathy, and cognitive control of emotions.

Forgiving is not easy—the need for taking revenge is hardwired in our system. In the past, that's how we prevented other people from causing us harm.

However, forgiveness is equally innate—reconciling after a fight is something most mammals do, not just humans. Reconciliation has an upside too. Research by the Stanford Forgiveness Project shows that forgiving elevates our mood and increases optimism.

I've learned through time and experience that resentment gets us nowhere. I usually don't hold a grudge on people—I don't want to be a prisoner of someone else's behavior.

I understand if you feel skeptical.

Researching for this article, I stumbled upon some compelling human stories. Some people went through the hardest experiences you can imagine. Yet, they were not only able to forgive but actually came in good terms with their wrongdoers.

Eva Kor, an Auschwitz survivor, publicly forgave the perpetrators who killed her parents and two older sisters at the camp. Eva even traveled to Germany and embraced Oskar Gröning, one of the Auschwitz officials.

Phyllis Rodriguez's son was killed in the World Trade Center attacks on September 11, 2001. Aicha el-Wafi's son was convicted of a role in those attacks and is serving a life sentence. In hoping to find peace, these two moms have formed a powerful friendship born of unthinkable losses.

Back in 1995, Azim Khamisa's son was killed in a gang initiation ritual. The deadly encountered sent him and Plex Felix, the grandfather of the murderer, down paths of meditation to forgive and be forgiven. In time, they became friends.

Unforgiveness is fueled by rumination—we keep rehashing bitter experiences. We get stuck on delated emotions. Resentment, hatred, hostility, fear, and anger guides our lives.

Blame and no forgiveness turns us into a victim—we feel helpless. If people who went through tragedies, as described above, forgave their offenders, why can't we?

Forgiveness doesn't mean forgetting. It's not accepting, justifying, or overlooking an event either. It's choosing to let go of resentment or the need for revenge—we eliminate the suffering, not the wrongdoing. The offender might not deserve your pardon, but you deserve to be at peace.

Time can help us heal, but forgiveness interventions work better.

Forgiving requires understanding.

Forgiving is an act of courage.

Like any behavior change, it requires a genuine commitment to succeed. The explicit decision to forgive someone is a critical step to move toward overcoming negative feelings.

Forgiveness sets you free from the past

When you forgive, you set yourself free.

**Learn how to forgive to seek the peace in soul**

# 7. SEED 7<sup>TH</sup>

## BE SUCCESSFUL

**"Success is only meaningful and enjoyable if it feels like your own." - Michelle Obama**

Each person has their own different opinion of success. To me, it's simple that success is to become a better version than yesterday.

Coming to recognize every gift and talent we possess within us takes a lifetime. Many of them surface during times of trial and difficult experience. Many surface as we gain more wisdom. Let's face it, we will likely never know everything we are truly capable of until life forces us to prove it to ourselves.

It is often said that "If you continuously compete with others, you become bitter, but if you continuously compete with yourself, you become better." We have to remind ourselves daily that our goal isn't to be better than anyone else. Our ultimate goal is to be better today than we were yesterday, and have a plan in place to help us become even better tomorrow

Recognize that every day we are the result of every past decision we have made up to that point. And tomorrow we are going to be the direct result of the decisions we are making today. So if we are doing things today that will make us better tomorrow, and we continue that pattern day after day, we are always going to be in the process of becoming our best. One way to do this is to ask yourself, "Where are the decisions I am making today going to lead me?" and, "Am I better today than I was yesterday?" and, "Do I have goals in place to help improve me tomorrow?

Some people say that success is to become the best person in the world, but In life there is no "superior" or "inferior" and there is no measuring stick that ranks us in order of importance. Everyone is exactly equal in importance to this world and it isn't possible for any one person to become more or less important than any other person. So then what do we aim for? How do determine excellence? How do we become "the best"?

We start by redefining what we believe "the best" is. We start by recognizing that being "the best" is something relating to you, and only you. It's about achieving your best, ranked solely against yourself and your own past performance and your own future potential. It's human nature to look for the grand slam and the quick-and-easy solution. But sometimes you just have to get on base and play the game, blocking and tackling your way to victory. As Ben Horowitz writes, there's no silver bullet that's going to turn your idea into a Fortune 500 overnight. What will work, however, is a lot of elbow grease and passion. You have to make opportunities for yourself and your company before you can make a profit.

Building a company and being an entrepreneur is all about constant improvement and sharing your story. This improvement isn't always instantaneous--it's often gradual and incremental. If you put in the work, tell your story, and focus on lead bullets rather than the silver, you'll be amazed at what you can accomplish simply by being a little better today than you were yesterday.

More beautiful, more intelligent, more successful

So what is the answer to achieving success in anything? Small steps that lead to constant improvement. Forget trying to lose those fifty pounds in a month. Instead, take baby steps and strive to be one percent better than yesterday. Start by exercising for one minute today, then slowly increasing the exercise duration each day, say by fifteen seconds. Write one hundred words of that book today and increase that by one percent the next day. Meditate for five minutes (300 seconds) today and add a mere three seconds tomorrow.

Slow and steady is the way to go when it comes to achieving your goals. There are no secret shortcuts or magical pills. The magic lies in making small, incremental improvements over time. All you need to do is to be one percent better than yesterday. That's it! A small, measly one percent! All of us can do that.

You may not see tangible results in the short run, but I guarantee you that you will see significant progress and results if you follow the one percent rule. One key point to remember is that, similar to placing your savings into a compounding interest bank account, the small successes will compound and lead to ever-increasing success levels. You will continuously build upon your previous success and the positive results will become exponentially more significant. The mistake that most people make is giving up early in the game when they do not detect tangible results.

Success is not a destination, it is an ongoing process. Successful people know that improving by a mere one percent each day leads to a 365% improvement over a year, and that is without any compounding! Just think about where you will be and the level of success you will attain if you simply improve by one percent each day. That is where the magic happens.

So, ask yourself this: how can you improve by one percent today?

**We take the gravel in the shell and we make a pearl**

# 8 SEED 8<sup>TH</sup>

## BE HAPPY

**"Learn to value yourself, which means: fight for your happiness."- Ayn Rand**

Happiness, what is it, and why do we strive to achieve it so persistently? Happiness in some points of view is portrayed as the state that is derived from self-awareness of a benefiting action or moment taking place. What of the moments that are not beneficial? Can a person still find moments of happiness and success in discord, a little glimmer of light shining from the deep recesses of our own consciousness? Plucking it from a mere moment.

Many times i wonder myself what is happiness and success. There I go drifting on my creative urges, but wait, that's what being successful is. The creative is the place where no one else has ever been. To get there one has to leave the city of comfort and go into the wilderness of the intuition. What is discovered is wonderful. Learning, telling stories, painting pictures, and sharing them with others, that's success. For the longest time I thought success was having a lot of money. So I worked, worked and then worked some more. I had money, but I had no time to do the things that made me really happy. Albert Schweitzer surmises, "Success is not the key to happiness, happiness is the key to success. If you love what you are doing, you will be successful." Real success is living a life of integrity, compassion and reciprocity.

Francis Bacon stated, "It's not what we eat but what we digest that makes us strong; not what we gain but what we save that makes us rich; not what we read but what we remember that makes us learned; and not what we profess but what we practice that gives us integrity." The ability to integrate positive and negative influences in one's life is the next step on the path to success. Success is a journey; it has multiple peaks, not one ultimate summit. One success builds another. Failures and setbacks are probably more important than success in these journeys. And success is a tasty part of happiness.

The only source of happiness – and unhappiness – comes from →
inside yourself. Happiness is an attitude. You either make yourself miserable, or happy. Choose to be happy. It is easy! Don't envy what others have and enjoy what you have, enjoy every moment of your life.

Don't wait for outer circumstances to make you happy, be happy now and always.

Learn to enjoy and enjoy learning. Keep smiling at your fate, and your fate will smile back at you.

"Jotting down just five things you're grateful for every day can lead to a healthier mental state…" Or at least this is what Julian Kesner from Prevention Magazine wrote in an article from 2008. Although happiness is something which is not yet measureable by science, most people would agree to experiencing happiness one or more times throughout their lives. Some people may even say they live in a state of happiness. Even though happiness is a relative state, people should follow through with the practice of being happy because happiness helps to keep people healthy, wealthy, and successful.
There is no denying that there is a direct correlation between being happy and being healthy.

People say that "Happy people have better moods, which means they make better decisions and feel able to rise to greater challenges." This statement suggests that happy people are more prone to being wealthy, because better decisions brings about better circumstances and a more direct route to being successful and wealthy. When the word wealth is used most people think of monetary wealth, but if the topic is happiness then other forms of wealth are to be considered as well. Wealth could be something tangible, such as money, things, or even a well-deserved promotion. However, wealth could also be things that make you feel enriched on an intangible level, such as time to spend with your family or the freedom to make your own choices with your future or success.

Happiness is the consequence of personal effort. You fight for it, strive for it, insist upon it, and sometimes even travel around the world looking for it. You have to participate relentlessly in the manifestations of your own blessings. And once you have achieved a state of happiness, you must never become lax about maintaining it. You must make a mighty effort to keep swimming upward into that happiness forever, to stay afloat on top of it."
— Elizabeth Gilber

Happiness is a easy choice

Happiness is an inner state of well-being and fulfillment, and therefore it has to come from inside. Every individual has his or her own emotions and way of thinking and as a result of this no one can really say what happiness is and what happiness is not. However, universally, happiness is a by-product of a healthy attitude and viewpoint. Happiness exists in everyone whether they choose to acknowledge and believe it or not. It is not rare nor is it something only the elite have: everyone has it but not everyone recognizes it. Contentment is finding a light at the end of every dark tunnel and in order to experience this we must ignore the pessimism surrounding us.

Looking back I had pleaded with my parents to allow me to enter before I was fully trained and my dejection on failing miserably was partly humiliation and partly realisation I was not fully prepared. Nevertheless, my love of horses and all things equestrian plays an immense role in my life to this day- complete contentment does not always stem from winning.

I once read "Happiness is a hundred choices. A thousand choices. All day long. Every day. Every year for the rest of your life". Happiness does not just happen, you choose how you will respond to everything; every situation, every person, everything. Subconsciously you decide between contentment or dejection. If you miss a bus do you go home? Or do you find a way to get to your destination? Or do you perhaps blame it on the fact you can't walk as fast as others? Happiness is not something life hands us and the key to happiness is choosing it. It is in these moments, however trivial or minor they are; you are choosing your life. Sometimes it is not a simple choice and more often than not it is something you have no desire to do. When woe strikes, it feels as though all you want to do is dwell on your sorrows. Some days are slightly more mediocre than others and some are just plain dreadful but your response to these days is of utmost importance. Sadness is a natural response to many things, but it is in no way compulsory behaviour. To be happy I believe you must change one thing.

In order to be truly happy, you should alter your attitude- not your life, but your point of view and outlook. Since I was young I have been told "Like it or not, life is not fair" and whilst I do agree life is not entirely fair, it's down to how you view it. Every one of us can choose to be either a pessimist and say the glass is half empty, or an optimist and say the glass is half full. Some people choose to live in a realm of negativity and pessimism without ever seeking to escape it. Being optimistic is a huge factor in happiness and whilst it is sometimes difficult to always be positive, it isn't impossible. As humans we are seasoned to negativity and society can often push it upon you and make you look on the black side of things. But finally, let's choose happiness which makes your life more fulfilling than ever before.

**Every day, I choose a fun for my soul**

# HAPPINESS IS

...following
your heart.

# 9. SEED 9TH

# LOVE

**"There is only happiness in this life, to love and to be loved."-George Sand**

Love is the master key that opens the gate of happiness.

It is amazingly simple to get that. You need to do just one thing – open your heart to love: love what you have; love what you do, and love other people.

What does love mean?
 This is another romantic quote which I believe can also be applied to other situations in our lives. As we have discussed before, the word "love" has a very wide range of meanings.
Yes, I believe that the love of a person qualifies for this quote, but not just romantic love. Those of you who are parents can probably remember a time, however brief, when your love of your children brought you to the gates of happiness.

Love of an ideal or a concept also qualifies, at least in my opinion. Love of freedom or justice can also bring you to the gates of happiness. And I believe that love of your fellow man can do so as well.

But, as always, you have to do a little work as well. Love gets you to the gates of happiness, but you must choose to go in, and then take action.

Many people seem to spend an inordinate amount of time standing in front of the wide-open gates of happiness, but hesitate to enter. I imagine you know some people like that. And at times, I have been that person myself.

Standing on the outside, peeking in, between the bars of the gate can become a bit of a habit. Other times, we get so used to not being able to get in, that when we the gate opens, we don't really know how to react.

But when opportunity knocks, we have to be ready to go. We must be prepared to step forward and avail ourselves of whatever opportunity has presented to us.

Regardless of what the opportunity might be, if we decline to step forward nothing will come of it, and opportunity will turn away from us. The quote says that love opens the gate to happiness, but we must be willing to step forward.

Where can I apply this in my life?

I hope you noticed that the quote does not say that love will magically cause happiness.

Love simply provides happiness the opportunity to present itself to you. There have been plenty of TV shows and movies which include a grumpy old man, one who has the love of friends or family. Yet for some reason, he won't step forward and through the gates of happiness.

Most of us do the same thing from time to time. It might be out of fear of the unknown, or comfort with present position or condition. It might not occur to us that we could, or should, take that step forward. Or we might feel unworthy of such happiness. It happens.

Awareness of opportunity helps, as does a bit of self-esteem. But above all else, action is required. In the taking of the step forward, we allow the feelings of happiness and pleasure in our bodies, in our mind, and in our spirit to flow through us.

Why Happiness is Your Secret to Productivity?

How are happiness and productivity related?

If you want to improve productivity, look no further than your mindset.

Marcus Aurelius reminds us:

"Very little is needed to make a happy life; it is all within yourself, in your way of thinking."

People who enjoy what they do are far more productive than those who do not have passion for their work. Have you ever been so engrossed in what you are doing that when you look up, you discover hours have passed in what seems like minutes? Such joyful immersion is the key to productivity. Everyone, regardless of gender and social status wants to be happy, to love and to be loved.

Unfortunately, not everybody succeeds because it is often that we either love or love us. So the question is unconscious: what is better – to love or to be loved?

It is difficult for a person to live without love

When a person loves and not, he feels unhappy. Okay, if you realize that it is impossible to make another person fall in love.

After all, the heart will not command. Therefore, one has to live by the fact that the person you love can ever love it.

But despite this, he wants to care for him, to do him good, but one who does not respond to love is usually unable to appreciate the kindness and gratitude of a loving heart.

Therefore, when two people meet and at first glance love each other, one of the greatest wonders of life is considered.

You understand that you can't go on any longer, but you can't do anything with yourself. But even then, positive things can be found. After all, your heart is full of love.

And love, as you know, makes man better, softer, more sensitive. It is difficult for a person to live without love. And when a person loves, let and without response, he feels different. First of all, a loving person looks at life in a completely different way.
Both love others and yourself as well.

Love what you do and do what you love.

DON'T
COUNT
THE DAYS.
MAKE
THE DAYS
COUNT.

# 10. SEED 10<sup>TH</sup>

## BE FREE

**"Be free, and live life fully."- Caroline Shaw**

Back to the olden days, women were confined at home to be a full-time housewife and their spouse were the single bread-winner for the family. It has become a mind frame for the public that women should not be allowed to work as their primary roles were to carry out domestic role and nurture their children. However, women certainly have their hidden potentials which make them capable as the opposite sex. Women should be allowed to work. This can be proven through intensive research and analysis. Based on the research that was conducted, some discoveries were made. Foremost, working women are found to have improvised self-esteem and emotional health due to their multiple roles in everyday lives. Next, job has secured them financially to sustain life. Last of all, women have their rights to step into labour force for personal satisfaction and social necessities. People have to perceive in wider context and accept the fact that women should be allowed to work as women can mould their lives with a sense of empowerment. Discrimination and inequality towards women should be stamped out to preserve their rights for them to unleash their concealed potentials.

Since centuries ago, people have being questioning what the distinctive role of women. In the past, women in the past were inferior to men in various aspects. However that does not halt women from showing the world they are stronger and more capable than they were many years ago. Women had strived hard to discard the biased stereotype of restriction of women to household responsibilities and duties. Outstanding women such as Queen Elizabeth II and Queen Russia the Great are excellent figur of s of women role models. As for this research, it examines and focuses on how people perceive the idea of "women should be allowed to work instead of staying at home".

In this modern era, people involved in labor force to gain monthly source of income for meeting daily necessities. Women are not exceptional too. In fact in America, the number of working women is escalating annually. They participate in work force for money to sustain family financially. However, women in this present day able to perceive beyond the benefits of working. Labour participation has helped them to feel a sense of achievement and pride apart from boosting their self-esteem and confidence.

The society should discard their old mindset that women should stay at home instead of working. Women are capable of successfully achieving what men can do. Besides, it is a right for women to work and earn money as what men can do. Although they play multiple roles of being mother, wife, daughter, sister and nonetheless being worker, they are still able to manage their domestic duties and parenting. This research focuses on benefits gained by working women instead of being full-time homemaker.

Hence, it is time that the public should grip to the statement that "women should be allowed to work" and support those independent women who want to make own living by working. Provided with strong arguments and evidences, the public should accept the fact that it is preferable for women to work and uncover their hidden potentials than sitting at home parenting and homemaking.

As other girls today, try your best to be free in life. It does not matter what your life looks like to anyone else. Their validation does not give your life value. Their admiration will never make you feel loved. The only thing outside approval will do is create pressure on you to keep being more, more, more.


It can be far too easy to convince yourself that your life must be valuable and special and worthwhile and glittery if someone else thinks so. Sometimes it seems like achieving outside approval is easier than giving ourselves the inner respect we all deserve to pursue. Because, there are ways and means that a culture will give you which will lead you to what others believe is an enviable life. Money. Labels. Cars. Shiny love. Shiny friends. Shiny things. These things look like a life that is worth something, at least that's what our consumerist and image-based culture has fed us for years. It's easy to gain approval. There's a road map. Just follow someone else's lead. Do the things you should do. Look the way you should look. Buy the things you should buy. Go to the things you should go to. Be the person you should be. Voila, ready-made validation!

The thing is, you can follow all the should until you're breathless and exhausted and in the middle of your breakdown or numb and purposeless and frustrated—which will happen, of course—and what you will never find at the end of the Rainbow Of Should's is self-fulfillment, self-respect, a self-prescribed life. If you chase the opinion of others to validate your life, you will do so forever. It will never end. There will always be more people to impress. You will never be enough, because there will always be a way to find your inadequacies—simply because you are searching for them. The system of needing external validation is set up to fail. It's set up to keep you running in a hamster wheel, over and over and over.

You must define your life. You have to be the last and final word of what your fulfilling life looks like. Outside validation is a prison you will live inside forever if you do not break that cycle. Nobody needs to live inside your life except you. You damn well better like what you've created. You damn well better enjoy who you are. It doesn't matter if anyone likes you or loves you or thinks you're worth big things or big dreams or big opportunities because, unless you see those parts of yourself, too, you will sabotage it. You will fuck it up. If you do not believe you are worth a big life, how could you ever enjoy it if you get it? If you don't even know—for yourself—what a big life looks like, how will you know when you have it?

The only way to affirm your life is for you to affirm it. The only way your life can be big or interesting or adventurous or filled with love is if you can recognize when it is. You can only recognize these things when you know what they look like. And, if you're too busy scrambling around for the admiration of others, you have no idea how to create your own life for yourself. You can create the vision of someone else's beautiful life or you can become aware of your own vision. One road leads to a never-ending cycle of needing the love of others to feel loved. The other allows you freedom to be and expand and define for yourself what makes you happy about your life.

It can feel like you will never be enough and, in many ways, you're right. You won't ever be enough if your enoughness lies in the hands of others. But, if you let yourself be enough now, in this moment, and you stop needing other people to affirm you, then you are free. When you take back the definitions and the labels and the little validations you seek on a daily basis, you realize you were imprisoned to other people's definitions of you and having to continue to either live those up or down. And, when you realize that your happiness and peace of mind was in the hands of strangers and friends and family members and lovers, then you can begin to take it back, piece by piece, until you're the only one in control of your happiness and peace of mind. That's freedom. That's ultimate freedom.

When you are the arbiter of your own life and you have no one to answer to except yourself, you are free. Not because you have escaped your life or fled the country or done anything other than the not-so-small feat of reclaiming what your life means to you and giving yourself the only affirmation you need. Freedom is not a place. It's not a shedding of responsibility or people or work or anything like that. It's inside you. You can either imprison yourself to the mind of a world that will continue to tell you that you are not enough and that you need to do more to prove you are more or you can free yourself. You can decide your life is enough right now. You can decide what a big, happy, juicy, beautiful life looks like and you can inch closer toward that.

That's true freedom.
**To be free doing what you like.**

# ABOUT THE AUTHOR

Jameka Watkins is the New York Times bestselling author of The Joy of Leaving Your Sh*t All Over the Place. She is also the author of Cocktails for Drinkers, Poetry from Scratch and the novel Afloat. Her work has appeared in the Atlantic, Teen Vogue and on BBC Radio 4.